The Second Edition of

LETTERS TO LITHOPOLIS

FROM O. HENRY
TO MABEL WAGNALLS

Issued by the Friends of the O. Henry Museum on the occasion of the naming of The O. Henry House and Museum as the first Texas Literary Landmark by the Center for the Book of the Friends of the Library, USA, a project of The Library of Congress, November 5, 1999.

*Fourth Annual Keepsake Publication of the
Friends of the O. Henry Museum*

*Limited edition
November 1999*

with introductory material by
Elmer Kelton
and Friends of the O. Henry Museum

First Printing Doubleday, Page & Company, 1922

Copyright © 1999
By Friends of the O. Henry Museum,
Austin, Texas

Published in the United States of America
By Eakin Press
A Division of Sunbelt Media, Inc.
P.O. Drawer 90159 Austin, Texas 78709-0159
email: eakinpub@sig.net
website: www.eakinpress.com

ALL RIGHTS RESERVED.

2 3 4 5 6 7 8 9

1-57168-355-0

For CIP information, please access:

FOREWORD

One of the first books I ever bought, at the high price of $2.49, was *The Complete Works of O. Henry*, its 1,653 pages containing all the previously published stories and poems of William Sydney Porter. Back in those happy if somewhat nervous college days, I was studying to become a writer myself, and I knew no one whose short stories I liked better than those of O. Henry.

As a youngster I first became enamored of the author because of his hilarious *The Ransom of Red Chief*, about the hapless kidnappers who steal a rich man's son but end up paying the father to take him back.

The problem I found in using O. Henry's stories as a model was that they were already falling out of fashion in the early 1940s. Teachers were critical of the surprise endings so typical in his work. They accused the stories of being shallow and built around gimmicks. In retrospect, it seems to me they were so wrapped up in diagnosing the plots that they missed the rich characterizations, the sparkling use of language. O. Henry at his best was a master stylist, a superb artist who painted brilliant pictures with words instead of a brush.

Foreword

Always sympathetic to the common man, he was at home writing about life in New York, in middle America, or in the cow camps of the Southwest. He dealt in a wide range of human experience: humor, drama, stark tragedy.

His letters to Mabel Wagnalls reflect his sharp wit, the playfulness which typified so many of his stories. But O. Henry was capable of presenting the dark underside of life as in his stories of unlucky big-city shop girls working for a pittance, or the grim vengeance of the Cisco Kid. He had a fine sense of irony, as in his *A Cosmopolite in a Café*, wherein his blasé man-of-the-world proves himself to be as provincial as those he has scorned for their narrow-mindedness.

The short story, once the most popular of literary forms, has fallen on hard times. Once the mainstay of dozens of fiction magazines, it began a rapid decline in the 1950s under the impact of television. It is a pity that so little short fiction is being published today. The world is richer for our having had O. Henry as one of its leading practitioners. A resurrection is definitely in order.

Elmer Kelton

Prologue from
ROADS OF DESTINY

I go to seek on many roads
    What is to be.
True heart and strong, with love to light—
Will they not bear me in the fight
To order, shun or wield or mould
    My Destiny?

Unpublished Poems
of David Mignot.

Three leagues, then, the road ran, and turned into a puzzle. It joined with another and a larger road at right angles. David stood, uncertain, for a while, and then took the road to the left. . . .

Whither those roads led he knew not. Either way there seemed to lie a great world full of chance and peril.

INTRODUCTION TO
THE SECOND EDITION

In April 1903, "Roads of Destiny" was published. Many readers were intrigued by the plot—a young French poet came to a crossroads and hesitated before taking one, which led to his death. But the plot was not over. In the second part of the story he was back at the crossroads, but he took another road—with the same result. Part three—the third choice led to the same ending. When Mabel Wagnalls read the story, she, too, was intrigued by the plot, but even more, she was captivated by the name "O. Henry" given as the name of the writer.

Many other readers were curious about the new author with just one initial before his name, but Miss Wagnalls, from her rather privileged position as the daughter of the Wagnalls of the publishing firm of Funk and Wagnalls, decided to find out about the writer whose name she described as being just a name with "an exclamation before it." She began to try to find out something about the person and the name—but that is all in Miss Wagnall's own introduction, which follows.

By that time, of course, many readers—and a

Introduction

number of publishers—had discovered the exciting writer who had suddenly burst upon the New York scene. He was so much in demand that he published simultaneously in several magazines during the same month, often under several "noms de guerre" as he labeled the varied names he used to conceal his true persona—and his past. But he was still unknown as a person to most of the public. From the readiness with which he responded to Miss Wagnall's letter it seems apparent that he was fascinated by her writing style—which reveals both naiveté and her own clever use of language—and perhaps by her availability as a literate correspondent. Or, perhaps it was, as she attributed it, his own shyness and loneliness. She says:

> *"A timid stranger"—somehow that describes him. To life itself and the whole world he carried the air of a timid stranger. . . . Never quite at home—just a little out of place—. . .*

In some ways, the letters that followed revealed much about the man behind the stories—although he purposely concealed the details of his identity. It was not until he had met Mabel and her mother in person that he corrected some of the fiction he had written into his letters. The two letters in which each confesses to the guilt brought on by their lack of complete openness are among the more charming segments of the correspondence.

Introduction

The reader familiar with O. Henry's later stories will recognize phrases and ideas he might have been trying out for effect: double meanings of words such as "bay," which he employed with effect much later (in "Two Thanksgiving Day Gentlemen") when Stuffy Pete in slicing the turkey, "carved for himself ... a crown of imperishable bay" (a pun on the meaning of "bay" as "laurel" and seasoning).

Also significant are the suggestions he gives her for looking at her surroundings and reporting on them—he was coaching her to be a better observer and hence a better writer, although she was already a published writer, her first book having been published ten years earlier when she was but twenty-one.

Thus her summer must have taken on an interest she might not otherwise have found, as well as contributing to her own sense of style. For example, her report of her earlier description of Lithopolis, written of course long after her mentor was gone, reflects some of his way of looking at America in terms of European tradition as well as reflecting in other details his playful way of looking at life.

> *... Lithopolis stands alone, maintaining an aloofness, an exclusiveness, that is unmatched ... by any other cluster of frame houses radiating around a one-block trading area of single-story shops. Not even the famous walled-in town of Rothenburg is so difficult to enter and so difficult to get out of after you're in.*

Introduction

In her explanatory notes, Mabel explains why the letters were not published until 1922, twelve years after Mabel and her mother joined the mourners at the funeral of O. Henry at the Little Church Around the Corner. The volume was published in a limited edition of 427.

In 1925 the eighteen-volume Biographical Edition of O. Henry's works was published. The introduction to the first of two volumes titled *Roads of Destiny* contained notes by Channing Pollock and Mabel Wagnalls, the latter a reprinting of Mabel's Introduction, labeled simply, *"Letters to Lithopolis,"* but the letters are not included.

As far as we have been able to establish, this is the first reprinting of the whole little volume, *Letters to Lithopolis,* in its entirety. The Friends of the O. Henry Museum offer this edition as the fourth in the series of Monographs. This edition is as nearly as possible a reprinting in the style of the original. We appreciate the care of Ed Eakin and the staff of Eakin Press in making this edi-tion a restoration of its seventy-seven-year-old model.

We are also most appreciative of a gift from Mr. James E. Scoggans, whose generous donation of an uncut version of the original edition brought the little book to the attention of the Friends of the Museum.

The day of issue of this edition is a happy one for fans of O. Henry and those who are seeking to keep his work known to a public for which it is ever fresh: the designation of the Austin O. Henry home and museum as the first Literary Landmark in Texas by

Introduction

the Center for the Book of the Friends of the Library, USA, a project of The Library of Congress. Dedication of a plaque describing the significance of the little house in the heart of modern Austin comes at the beginning of the Book Festival, which is bringing many current writers to the city and recognizing their contributions to American literature at the end of the century, as O. Henry contributed to literature at its beginning.

> by Vi Marie Taylor, Chair
> Friends of the O. Henry Museum
> November 5, 1999

Paul S. Clarkson. A Bibliography of William Sydney [sic] Porter (O. Henry). Caldwell, Idaho: The Caxton Printer, Ltd. 1938.

LETTERS TO / LITHOPOLIS / FROM O. HENRY / TO / MABEL WAG-NALLS / (Publisher's device) / GARDEN CITY, N.Y., AND TORONTO / DOUBLEDAY, PAGE & COMPANY / 1922

LETTERS TO LITHOPOLIS and the Publisher's device are printed in red ink.

Backstrip reads: LET / TERS / TO / LITHO / POLIS / FROM / O. / HEN / RY / TO / MABEL / WAG / NALLS / DOUBLEDAY PAGE & CO. (in two vertical columns) / MCMXXII—in four of eight panels, each with a single-rule gilt border and each separated by three rules in gilt.

Size: 8vo: ($7^{11}/_{16}$" x 5"). Size of pages: $7^5/_8$" x $4^7/_8$", with top edge trimmed, other edges untrimmed. Signatures: in eights.

Collation: Plain brown end paper; (i), stating: THIS EDITION IS LIMITED TO FOUR / HUNDRED AND TWENTY-SEVEN COPIES OF / WHICH THREE HUNDRED AND SEVENTY- / SEVEN ARE FOR SUBSCRIBERS IN THE / UNITED STATES, AND FIFTY FOR SUB- / SCRIBERS IN ENGLAND. / NO. ____; verso (ii), blank; (iii), half title; verso (iv), blank; (v), title (as above); verso (vi): Copyright, 1922, by Doubleday, Page & Company, etc.; vii-xxix, Preface; verso (xxx), blank; (xxxi), subtitle; verso (xxxii), blank; 1-58, text; 59: Publisher's statement and colophon; verso (60), blank; plain brown end paper.

Binding: Half vellum, with stiff brown wrappers over boards. Front cover has LETTERS / TO LITHOPOLIS / FROM / O. HENRY / TO MABEL WAGNALLS stamped in gilt within a blind-stamped panel measuring $2^{13}/_{16}$" x $1^1/_2$", surrounded by a gilt-stamped box 3" x $1^5/_8$".

Thickness of the book, with covers, is $^1/_2$". Thickness of pages is $^5/_{16}$".

LETTERS TO LITHOPOLIS

FROM
O. HENRY
TO
MABEL WAGNALLS

LETTERS TO LITHOPOLIS

FROM O. HENRY
TO
MABEL WAGNALLS

GARDEN CITY, N. Y., AND TORONTO
DOUBLEDAY, PAGE & COMPANY
1922

COPYRIGHT, 1922, BY
DOUBLEDAY, PAGE & COMPANY

ALL RIGHTS RESERVED, INCLUDING THAT OF TRANSLATION
INTO FOREIGN LANGUAGES, INCLUDING THE SCANDINAVIAN

PRINTED IN THE UNITED STATES
AT
THE COUNTRY LIFE PRESS GARDEN CITY, N. Y.

PREFACE

"The human Will, that force unseen,
　The offspring of a deathless Soul,
　Can hew a way to any goal,
Though walls of granite intervene."

IT is always a privilege to meet a great man. The revelation of him when off-guard and not busied with fashioning either forms or fancies for the public eye is sure to radiate some flash of personality that is inspiring. There are just two methods of encountering genius away from the limelight—by a handshake or a letter. The handshake and exchange of words may be eternally impressive—to one person; but to meet, in the pages of a letter, with one of these soaring spirits—one whose altitude is measured by the depth of

PREFACE

his insight—this is an exhilaration that may be shared with others. My first meeting with O. Henry was of this sort, and the thrill of astonishment I received I am enabled to pass on to every reader of this little book. The experience, surprising as it was delightful, had a prelude I must explain.

Some months before, I had read a story that greatly impressed me; it was "Roads of Destiny." Not only was I impressed by the originality of the idea and style, but also by the originality of the author's name. Just "Henry" with an exclamation before it. I wondered how a writer could hope to be remembered with such a casual tag-mark. What superb indifference to fame! Then, on second thought, I considered it a clever bid for fame—a name so coy as to be conspicuous. Then, on third

PREFACE

thought, that Henry name began to stir up activities in other crevices of my brain. I had a great grandmother named Henry. Our family tree I had long since discovered to be sadly lacking in decorations. No stars or coronets hung on its boughs, nor even a horse-thief to vary the respectable monotony. Perhaps here was an offshoot I had missed—a Henry branch that might prove illustrious. I searched in "Who's Who" and asked literary friends, but "O. Henry" was on no list of celebrities I could find. So I scribbled a few lines to his publisher, told who I was —or rather who my father was—and, as one publisher to another, so to speak, I begged to know whether O. Henry was man, woman, or wraith.

I mailed the missive—and forgot it. Time—but why be prosaic? "The

PREFACE

days," to quote from my favourite author, "with Sundays at their head, formed into hebdomadal squads, and the weeks, captained by the full moon, closed ranks into menstrual companies carrying Tempus Fugit on their banners."

By the time Thirty-fourth Street was displaying sport suits and parasols and the trunk stores were announcing instant removals, my mother and I made our annual visit to my grandmother's home in Lithopolis. You have possibly never heard of this town. Don't look for it on the map: it isn't there. And don't look for it from any railroad train window: it isn't there, either. Lithopolis stands alone—faithfully guarding an ancient stone quarry so long disused that no one knows when it last was drilled or blasted. Again let me say that Lithopolis stands

PREFACE

alone, maintaining an aloofness, an exclusiveness, that is unmatched, I believe, by any other cluster of frame houses radiating around a one-block trading area of single-story shops. Not even the famous walled-in town of Rothenburg is so difficult to enter and so difficult to get out of after you're in. The daily mail-wagon was, at the time of our visits there, the sole public means of transit thither and thence; and likewise the one excitement of the day.

There are three hundred and fifty inhabitants in Lithopolis—never more, never less. The two hundred and eight houses it contains are kept in repair, and even rebuilt, but a new house is never added. Rather than do this people leave the town— or die. It is cheaper. People never move to Lithopolis, but they can't help being born there. This is what

PREFACE

happened to both my father and mother. Lithopolis is *élite* as the St. Nicholas Club of Manhattan: to belong to it you must be born to it. And, by way of further resemblance, its people are eternally clannish; they have a way of clinging to the home-town with a fondness that is irrefutable. Though the place is small and primitive, the surrounding hills are delightful, and the near-by ravine, with its winding stream, would thrill the heart of a Corot. The inhabitants are neighbourly and on good terms with one another in spite of the paling fences that divide off their front yards. Flowers grow near every doorway, and at the end of Main Street, up on the hill, is a picturesque graveyard shaded by stately elms and spruce that give it an impressive dignity.

There is a tinge of old-world aris-

PREFACE

tocracy in the town's disdain for all phases of modern industry. Reposeful as a medieval princess in a rockbound castle, Lithopolis takes no heed of the whirring wheels and high-pressure mechanism of the outer world. The little community is almost self-sustaining. In its straggling business block you will find, besides the general store, a drug store—that indulges in literature on the side, a barber's shop—very active on Saturday evenings, and a butcher's shop that never saw a filet or a tenderloin. There is a millinery shop that cuddles close to the post office, and just beyond the second lane sounds a blacksmith's shop. The hardware store plies a good trade in plows— and also deals in coffins. There are four churches to say prayers over the coffins when they are filled, and on the other street (there are only two)

PREFACE

is the shop of a tombstone-maker (her name is Alta Jungkurth—more of her later). And opposite to this shop stands the house and surrounding trees, the little garden and chicken corral of my eighty-year-old grandmother whose mother had been born a Henry.

Though the outlook from my grandmother's window was a bit doleful, the Lutheran church right adjoining imparted an atmosphere of peace and strength that enabled us to contemplate the tombstones across the way with equanimity. One grew quite accustomed to them, in fact. As new monuments were frequently erected in the graveyard to replace less pretentious ones, the discarded old stones became an accumulation. Whenever a good flat-surfaced slab was needed for any sort of purpose the neighbours knew where to ask

PREFACE

for it. Mrs. Needles decapitated her chickens on a stout piece of slate that bore a worn inscription to Ezekiel Smith, born 1803—died 1810. Another neighbour's front doorstep, had you peered underneath, told of one Hermann Baumgarten, who left this world in 1842.

All things were conducive to making my grandmother's home a peaceful place in which to dream dreams and put them into words. For this purpose I used to resort to the attic —a huge space with slanting roof, and to my mind the best furnished region in the house. There was a spinning wheel, and several old chests (one had a secret drawer), and, most eerie of all, was a huge-faced, highly decorated clock, decrepit and out of use, that stood on the floor. This clock had an uncanny way of striking One at rare intervals, apparently for

PREFACE

no reason at all, though we finally concluded that some unnoticed jarring of the floor must have occasioned it. An apple tree bough, close to the house, swept across one of the attic windows. In the spring, when this bough was abloom and the window was open—ah!—it was a place for any sort of wild fancy to unfold.

Secreted one day in my precious attic, I had seated myself on the floor by a chest, where I was scribbling energetically and picturing myself as a starving poet forced to dwell near the eaves, when I heard the voice of my mother:

"Come down, Mabel; here's a letter from Henry!"

I had a distant cousin by this name from whom letters were frequent and I was puzzled at the special summons to read a letter from him. Again she called:

PREFACE

"From Henry, the author." Whereupon I said "O!" I came down and was soon reading aloud the jolliest, breeziest, most unusual letter that had ever come my way.

After several re-readings to the entire household, there loomed before me the prospect of replying to this post-impressionist epistle. How to answer this answer to my query about "O. Henry" was a problem. But I didn't go up to the attic to do it. I drew the old Boston rocker up to my grandmother's big centre table, shoved back the Bible, the family album, and the lamp, and soon pushed my pen easily enough into the opening sentence with the natural statement that his letter had been forwarded to Lithopolis. Then, as day follows night, as ferment follows yeast, that name "Lithopolis" had to be explained. It is a name never

PREFACE

mentioned to the uninitiated without eliciting a circle of questions, so I put down, then and there, all that seemed to me needful about the cosmopolis Lithopolis. After dinner I handed the letter over the fence to Nellie Laney (the postmistress) on her way up street to sort the noon mail.

Not long after this there was another red-letter day in the little house next to the Lutheran church; eight pages of uproarious manuscript from my mysterious, ink-slinging, Texas-cowboy correspondent sojourning in New York were read aloud to my mother and grandmother, the hired girl and the cat, to say nothing of a neighbour or two (O. Henry's reputation was growing!). And right then, as I read those rollicking pages, I realized that Lithopolis had occasioned them. I realized this fact more and more as his letters con-

PREFACE

tinued to come. His publishers realize it to-day: hence the title on the cover of this book. A little old, obscure town it is, unfitted for any highway place along the roads of steel. In a quiet nook on "Roads of Destiny" is where you will find Lithopolis. A great mind and spirit, speeding on to fame, found time once to note and give heed in his letters to the side-tracked tiny town.

O. Henry, unheralded as yet, a lone stranger in New York, evidently found enough diversion in my Lithopolitan news-letters to impel him to continue making use of the Pennsylvania and Hocking Valley Railroads, in conjunction with two horses and a mail-wagon, as carriers for some high-grade samples of the World's Best Literature. It required no exceptional genius on my part to realize that his letters were worth saving. I

PREFACE

kept them at first in my desk; then in a letter file; then (my precaution keeping pace with his fame) in a tin box; and finally they were handed over to my father who had suggested placing them in his safe at the office. This he did—unmindful of the fact that that particular safe had an uncanny reputation for discriminating judgment in the matter of priceless mementos. It was the same safe that had swallowed up and concealed for years Dr. Funk's famous "Widow's Mite"—an incident that required a whole book to explain. That safe now promptly made away with our precious O. Henry letters, and in spite of much frantic search for them, the little shelf where they had been, where they should have been, and where they certainly were placed—was a shelf blankly innocent of any papers bearing the Henry

PREFACE

chirography. So great was our amaze at the wraith-like Houdini, the lock-conquering break-away of those letters, that at first I felt, as their author has said, "there could be no more calendar, neither days, weeks, nor months."

But time sped firmly on, not only months but years. And during those years, O. Henry's fame grew. Oh, how it grew! The whole world knew this, but none knew it better, none knew it so deeply, as my mother and I and Daddy—especially Daddy! We read columns and pages in the papers about O. Henry, and always we finished with the wail, "What a pity about those letters!" It did seem as though an unmerciful amount of news about America's greatest humourist came our way. Friends, aware of my acquaintance with him, took pains to send me clippings. It

PREFACE

finally became an unwritten law of our home to avoid the mention of his name, for the memory of those lost letters was too exasperating.

Still more years flocked by. Then one day came a voice over the telephone: my father from his office shouting good news: "I have found the O. Henry letters!" It is not clear to me yet how he found them, or where; apparently in some nook as obscure in that safe as Lithopolis is on the map. Anyway, here they are, and I truly believe every reader will receive the same thrill they imparted to us when first read aloud, long ago, in my grandmother's cosy front room.

My acquaintance with O. Henry, as an occasional caller in our New York home, leaves the memory of a quiet, serious, hard working author; one whom I felt was predestined to

PREFACE

fame though he had slight regard for the author-craft. He was sincere in his statement of belief that "writing pieces for the printer isn't a man's work." His idea of a man's work was to get out in the world and establish a great business—as John Wanamaker did. Several times I heard him speak with profound admiration of this merchant prince, whom he had never met. Equally sincere, I have good reason to believe, was his expressed indifference to music; he never asked me to play. I served tea and cakes when he called and we talked casually on any subject under the moon. I told him how his first letter reached me when I was up in the attic trying to imagine myself a poor, starving poet. I can hear yet his prompt and serious reply.

"That is something you cannot imagine. No one who has not known it

PREFACE

can imagine the misery of poverty." O. Henry was so serious in saying this his voice became almost tragic. "Poverty is so terrible and so common, we should all do more than we do—much more—to relieve it. We intend to, perhaps, but we don't do it. You ought to do more, so ought I, right now. I ought to give fifty dollars, but I don't." Though making a social call, O. Henry was just then deeply solemn and earnest. Was he ever jocose in his talk as in his writings? I never found him so. About the only witticism I recall was the last time I saw him; the very last words I heard from him. As he stood at the door after saying good-bye he asked whether he might come again, real soon. I laughingly asked what he called "real soon."

"What time do you have breakfast?" was the merry retort.

PREFACE

Shortly after this my mother and I went to Europe and it chanced that we never again saw O. Henry. But some time later he sent, through my father's office, his most recent book with an inscription highly typical and dashed off in his best freehand style:

"*To Miss Mabel Wagnalls—*
  with pleasant recollections of a certain little tea party where there were such nice little cakes and kind hospitality to a timid stranger.
                    O. HENRY."

"A timid stranger"—somehow that describes him. To life itself and the whole world he carried the air of a timid stranger. Something in his manner made me think of William Watson's "World Strangeness":

PREFACE

"Strange the world about me lies,
    Never yet familiar grown—
Still disturbs me with surprise,
    Haunts me like a face half-known.

. . . .

I have never felt at home,
    Never wholly been at ease."

So it seemed with O. Henry. Never quite at home—just a little out of place—and even in death—— But I must tell this very gently, and with somewhat of bated breath. We went to O. Henry's funeral, my mother and I. We had read in the papers of his passing, and had noted the hour and the place; a fitting place it was—the Little Church Around the Corner—the Church of the Strangers, as it sometimes is called. We supposed there would be a large crowd; probably cards of admission would be required. We had none, but we went intending to stand on the curb,

PREFACE

if need be, to pay our last deference to one of America's Immortals. But no crowd edged the curb; we saw a few carriages and a small group at the door that somehow was far from funereal in appearance. On entering the vestibule we were accosted with a question. So certain were we it must be a request for a card that for a moment we were uncomprehending —and good reason there was for our dismay. We had heard the strangest question ever worded, I believe, at chancel door since the cross of Christ stood over it:

"Have you come for the wedding or the funeral?"

Somehow it was a phrase that stabbed to the heart, though we soon understood, of course, that a mistake had been made in the time set for the two ceremonies. The wedding party was already there but it was decided

PREFACE

to hold the funeral first. So a few of us—astonishingly few, unbelievably few—sat forward in the dim nave while a brief—a very brief—little service was read over the still form of one whose tireless hand had penned pages of truth, humour, and philosophy that will live as long as the foundation stones of our Hall of Fame endure.

One felt a hurried pulse through all the service, and as the cortège passed out a flower or two fell from the casket and we knew that soon the bridal train would be brushing them aside. Out of place, it would seem, to the last, was O. Henry; with hardly time in the church to bury him. But his work, his books—there is place for them in four million homes of those who speak his tongue; more than four million copies of his books have been sold.

PREFACE

Yes, there is room in the world for his work. And there is room in the hearts of the people for his fame to rest for ever.

Mabel Wagnalls.

LETTERS TO LITHOPOLIS

FROM
O. HENRY
TO
MABEL WAGNALLS

LETTERS TO LITHOPOLIS

I

O. HENRY
TO MISS WAGNALLS

New York, June 9th, 1903.

MY DEAR MADAM:

THE "Cosmopolitan Magazine" forwarded to me *yesterday* the little note you wrote on May 9th, in regard to some of the short stories I have been perpetrating upon the public. I do not know why they held your letter so long unless they thought it was a MS. submitted for publication, and finally decided to reject it—in which case I think they showed very poor taste and judgment.

I'm glad to be able to tell you that I am a man, and neither a woman nor a wraith. Still I couldn't exactly

LETTERS TO

tell you why I'm glad, for there isn't anything nicer than a woman; and I have often thought, on certain occasions, that to be a wraith would be exceedingly jolly and convenient.

When you were looking for "O. Henry" between the red covers of "Who's Who" I was probably between two gray saddle blankets on a Texas prairie listening to the moonlight sonata of the coyotes.

Since you have been so good as to speak nicely of my poor wares I will set down my autobiography. Here goes!

Texas cowboy. Lazy. Thought writing stories might be easier than "busting" broncos. Came to New York one year ago to earn bread, butter, jam, and possibly asparagus that way. Last week loaned an editor $20.

Please pardon the intrusion of

LITHOPOLIS

finances, but I regard the transaction as an imperishable bay. Very few story writers have done that. Not many of them have the money. By the time they get it they know better.

I think that is all that is of interest. I don't like to talk about *l*iterature. Did you notice that teentsy-weentsy little "l"? That's the way I spell it. I have much more respect for a man who brands cattle than for one who writes pieces for the printer. Don't you? It doesn't seem quite like a man's work. But then, it's quite often a man's work to collect a cheque from some publications.

I was very glad to get your letter, even though it comes as to a wraith or an impersonality. Why? Well, down in Texas we are sort of friendly, you know, and when we see a man five miles off we holler at him "Hello,

LETTERS TO

Bill"! In New York the folks—well,—(I wish I could show you right here how the Mexicans shrug one shoulder). Your letter seemed to read like a faint voice out of the chaparral calling: "Hello, Bill, you old flop-eared wraith, how're they comin'?" In Texas the folks freeze to you; in New York they freeze you. Sabe?

But I do not consider this a fault in New York. After one gets acquainted with the people they prove to be very agreeable and friendly. I have made a number of friends among the magazine men whom I like very much.

What a pity it is that a downtrodden scribbler can't manage to claim kinship with a publisher's family! 'Way down in Louisiana is where my "Henry" name came from. Can't you dig up an ancestor among the

LITHOPOLIS

old Southern aristocracy so we can be cousins?

Do you know, Miss Wagnalls, what would be the proper procedure on this occasion if this happened to be Texas? I'll tell you. I'd get on my bronco and ride over to 15th Street and holler "Hello, folkses!" And your pa would come out and say: "Light and hitch, stranger"; and you would kill a chicken for supper, and we would all talk about *l*iterature and the price of cattle.

But as this is New York and not Texas I will only say I hope you will overlook the nonsense, and believe that I much appreciate your cheering letter. There are one or two stories that I think you have not seen that I would like to have your opinion of if you would let me submit them to you some time. I think the judgment of a normal, intelligent

LETTERS TO

woman is superior to that of an editor in a great many instances.

    Sincerely yours,
     O. HENRY.
      47 West 24th Street.

—

II

O. HENRY
TO MISS WAGNALLS

   New York, June 25, 1903.

MY DEAR MISS WAGNALLS:

YOUR pleasant little note from the metropolis Lithopolis was received and appreciated, although some envy was stirred up at the sight of your postmark. Just think!—you are out in the wilds of Ohio where you can pick daisies and winners at the county racetrack, wear kimonos and shoes large enough for you and run either for exercise or office as often as you please. Me—I'm in my

LITHOPOLIS

garret nibbling at my crust (softened by a little dry Sauterne) and battling with the wolf at the door—(he's trying to get out—don't like it inside).

Lemme see! Fairfield County—that's over across the "crick," isn't it, just this side of the woods? And Lithopolis—wait a minute—b'lieve I've heard of—— No, it wasn't the town—I guess it was a new $3 shoe or a trotting horse I was thinking of. (The whole paragraph was inspired by envy. I know it's peaceful & lovely & rural and restful out there. "Lost in Lithopolis; or Lolling among the Lotuses—not to mention the Lima Beans." 'Twould make a summer drama that would snow "The Old Homestead" under—paper snow, of course.)

Wait a minute—let me consult my notes—— Oh yes—— Thanks again for saying such kind things about my stories. But let's talk about something else—writing little pieces for the printer man isn't much. There ought to be a law reserving literature for one-legged veterans and widows with nine children to write. Men ought to have the hard work to do—they ought to read the stuff.

Er—lemme see—— Oh yes:—will I be wending my way back to Texas? (Please don't say "wending"; it has such a footsore, stone-bruisy sound to it. Makes you think of railroad ties and things.) Well, I dunno. Sometimes I get tired of New York, and want to be where I can holler "Hello, Aunt Emily!" to the mayor's wife, and go back of the counter in the post office with a sort of Lithopolitan insouciance and freedom. The other night I went up to the Madison Square post office and sat on the steps for two hours. Do

LITHOPOLIS

you know, that postmaster never even came out and said "how's tricks," much less joining in for a social chat. Everybody is so stiff in New York. But I hardly think I'll leave this year. I've got the editor men chasing me for stuff now, and I want to work 'em a while longer.

Now, let's see again—— Oh yes —am I interested in music? Now, I think right here is where you are going to repudiate your cousin, for I know all about why you asked the question. I can just see the dreamy look in your eyes as you slather Chopin and Bay Toven out of the piano keys. Am I interested in music?— Well, er—why, certainly—interested, but not implicated. I once was reputed to know something about printed music, but I acquired the distinction by fraud. I gained it by being able to stand at the piano and turn the music exactly at the proper time for a certain young lady, who aggravated the ivory frequently. No one ever found out that she gave me the signal by moving her right ear, a singularly enviable accomplishment that she possessed. I may say that I had an ear for music, but it did not belong to me.

I was going to send you a couple of old magazines with plot stories that I think would have interested you, but on looking I find that I haven't kept copies of them. I trespass so far on your good nature, though, to send 2 or 3 recent ones that you may not have noticed, as being afflicted with "O. H." stuff. I'll send you the July "McClure's" in a day or two (if I may) which contains another. I don't think that anybody but you reads them, and I don't want my audience to get away. I

LITHOPOLIS

am thinking of getting out a nice red book with chewed-up edges pretty soon, and I was feeling really hopeful and enthusiastic at the thought that you might buy a copy and thus enable it to appear in the list of most popular works sold in the Lithopolis department stores. But I reflected that as a member of a publisher's family you would be able to get one at wholesale rates, or maybe free, and the dream has faded.

I ought to apologize for writing so much, but it is such a comfort to send out MS & know that it will not be returned.

If you have time & sufficient charity I would like to hear something more about Lithopolis. How are the Domineck chickens getting along, and has your grandmother had the fence painted this spring?

Sincerely yours
O. Henry.

LETTERS TO

III

INTRODUCTORY NOTE

THE Dramatis Personae of the next letter requires some explaining and introducing. A play manager, glancing over the manuscript, would say there are too many characters. The list of names is indeed formidable and varied. They are here presented in the order of their appearance, as the up-to-date programs say:

Mr. E. J. Wheeler.

Don Hypolito Lopez Pomposo Antonio Riccardo Doloroso

  Otto
  Oliver
  Obadiah
  Orlando
  Oscar
  Orville
  Osric

LITHOPOLIS

Bart Kramer
The Tombstone Lady
Barefoot Boy
Bouncer

To begin at the beginning—consider the Top Liner, Mr. E. J. Wheeler. Why is he here? First of all he is not *Mr.* Wheeler—he is *Dr.* Wheeler (the Alma Mater kind). And he is not squat, square-faced, and distracted-looking; he is tall, dignified, and the epitome of poise. You can see his name, if you look for it, on the news-stands every month. (He is editor of a well-known magazine.) And you can hear his voice, if you go there, once a month, at the meetings of the Poetry Society, of which he is the Pioneer and Pilot. He is one of the literary friends I first turned to when seeking information about the creator of "Roads of Destiny." He it was, in fact, who suggested that I send a letter to the publisher. Dr. Wheeler was at one time associated with my father's firm. I know him well; so well, indeed, that I know his faults, though no very close acquaintanceship is needed to discover his principal failing. Dr. Wheeler is absentminded. It is not merely the absentmindedness of poetic frenzy. He did not become thus distinctive, he was always so, he was born so. The tales Mrs. Wheeler could tell—! Indeed, she was to be envied as a conversationalist, for she was steadily supplied with home-made, enlivening anecdotes; the Doctor always enjoyed these (after they happened) as much as she did. But knowing this propensity of his, I was in the habit of forestalling it, taking all due precaution against his forgetfulness when I approached him on any important

LITHOPOLIS

matter. It now occurred to me to let Dr. Wheeler know that I had unearthed the elusive author I was trailing, and to have them meet each other. For this purpose I sent my new friend a letter of introduction to the old one, and expressed a hope that he would present the letter before Dr. Wheeler forgot he was coming. (I was mailing at the same time a note to the Doctor explaining his prospective caller.) These precautions on my part are what stirred up O. Henry's artistic instinct to the point of picturing my absent-minded editor friend.

The second name on the list, Don Hypolito Lopez Pomposo Antonio Riccardo Doloroso, I am in no way responsible for. But the following three, Otto, Oliver, and Obadiah, are my own—my very own—I invented them. I have mentioned before my keen interest in the initial standing

LETTERS TO

sentry to that Henry name; that modest-violet sort of *nom de plume* that was, whether intended or no, a regular trumpet-call for attention so enticed and tantalized me that I did well to wait until my third letter before broaching the subject. I wasted no time in subtleties—just asked point-blank what the "O." stood for, and told him the only names I could think of were Oliver, Otto, and Obadiah. His reply was delightfully disconcerting. I could not charge him with ignoring my question; he must have given a full hour's work to the answer. But none the less, I was left in the air— with a subconscious feeling that someone had told me his front name was his own and would I kindly stay put in my grandmother's yard and not try to play in Madison Square. In a later letter I learned why O. Henry

LITHOPOLIS

stubbed his pen and could not answer when I asked him what the "O." stood for. The plain fact is it stands for just nothing—exactly as it does in our arithmetics at school. O. Henry had never bothered to devise a name for that "O." It stands there alone, and will stand so for ever, an unwitting emblem of his fame—that enduring circle, the symbol of eternity.

And now for Bart Kramer—ubiquitous Bart—who owned the barn that was burnt to the ground. This much he knows and must well remember, but that that fire was described to a lazy genius in New York who lit upon it as a subject for some clever pen strokes that eventually find themselves perpetuated in a book—all this will be news to Bart. It was a fine fire, lacking nothing in the way of spectacular effects—mid-

LETTERS TO

night—church bells ringing—all Lithopolis aroused, leaving its front doors open as it rushed to the blaze half-dressed. The roof was aflame when I arrived: we all brought utensils and formed a bucket brigade. Phil Oyler and Bart's brother Jake took turns at the pump, filling buckets, which were passed on from hand to hand to the blazing barn, where Bart himself was frantically emptying and handing them to another line of neighbours who passed them rapidly back to the panting pump. The frightened chickens and barking dogs added gloriously to the excitement. It did not last long and no one was hurt, and it certainly was, taken all in all, a perfectly lovely fire.

In the course of my lively but brief correspondence with O. Henry, I learned to rely on the Tombstone

LITHOPOLIS

Lady. Whenever Lithopolis seemed drained of incident and I found my pen lagging, I could always fall back upon Alta Jungkurth (she was muscular from her trade and could stand it). If your mind grasps at all the fact of a woman chiselling tombstones, you probably are picturing her as a middle-aged, frowsy-haired, masculine-appearing person, loud-voiced and assertive. Wipe out the picture—you will have to do it all over. Our Tombstone Lady was good-looking—yes, noticeably so—and soft-voiced, and at that time, I should say, full fifty years younger than the age at which according to Ecclesiastes she would have personal use for one of her own stones. She was tall, strong, and well-built, for her father had been a monumental man—so to speak. The music of the chisel (for the shop adjoined the

LETTERS TO

home) had been her first lullaby, and stones—everlasting stones—tall, short, round, square, cuneiform, and oblong; white, gray, and granite-red —stones were her only toys. She had occasional pets, a cat for one, but he died. His name was Tom, and Alta gave vent to her grief by erecting a stone to his memory—it stands to this day in the yard:

Here Lies
TOM
Alta Jungkurth's Cat

This is the simple inscription that serves to immortalize Tom, and also to prove that Alta started early at her trade. In course of time she became her father's sole assistant. When other girls were learning to embroider and trace monograms on fancy work they sent to the county fair, Alta was tracing letters upon

LITHOPOLIS

enduring stone, destined for display upon the hilltop. She became expert in marking off and chiselling all kinds of decorations—both the deep-cut and bas-relief. So what more natural than that she should take her father's place in the shop when he, at last, took his place in the graveyard. There were orders unfilled, stones already contracted for, to say nothing of the one now needed to carry the name of Jungkurth. Alta bared her strong right arm and went to work in earnest. She even understood the "setting 'em up"—which is not nearly so jocose a matter as it sounds in O. Henry's letter. There is a whole lot to learn and master in this unusual tombstone trade—certain law requirements about foundations, the underground depth of stone and cement. You hired day-labourers or the grave-digger for this work. But sometimes Alta pitched in and did most of it herself. Often have I seen her with swinging step returning from the graveyard balancing upon her shoulder a huge clay-encrusted spade. Sometimes she was red in the face and furious because her helpers did not do as she told them. I saw her once, in a temper, fling her spade across the yard and declare that no man in the world seemed to know enough to dig a straight line or set a foundation. She had, on this particular day, been obliged to undo what the men had done and rebuild it all herself. No one could deny that Alta knew the tombstone business from the ground up and from the surface down; so expert was she that for miles around she was often sent for to chisel all day in some quiet graveyard at a stone already erected. Indeed, I so ad-

LITHOPOLIS

mired her energy and unconscious hewing of new paths for woman's work that I wanted to write an article illustrated with pictures showing her at her unusual trade. This last suggestion shattered the project; to be pictured in her work clothes did not appeal to Alta. When she posed before the camera it must be in her Sunday best. With this dictum still clear in my memory, I look with relief upon the drawing O. Henry has made of her. I am sure it will not ruffle her feelings sartorially if she chances to see this book. M. W.

O. HENRY
TO MISS WAGNALLS

New York, July 23rd, 1903.

MY DEAR MISS WAGNALLS:

JUST for a change from the side view of the Lutheran Church and the "tombstone lady's" outfit across the

LETTERS

street, will you let me have the floor for a few lines? Thank you very much for your card of introduction to Mr. Wheeler, although I haven't allowed myself the pleasure of calling upon him. You neglected to inform me whether his office is in the second story or the sixth, and I'm shy about bearding absent-minded editors who live too high above the sidewalk. From long practice I am able to land safely out of a second-story window, but when I scrape an acquaintance I don't want it to be a skyscraper. I have a gifted imagination in some things—here's my idea of Mr. Wheeler from your description. It represents him in the act of trying not to forget to ring the bell when people call on him who do not write articles on "Social Inconsistencies of Compound Hypermatrophic Astigmatism." You will notice that my

O. Henry's "idea of Mr. Wheeler"

LETTERS

reluctance to beard editors has led me to give Mr. Wheeler a perfectly smooth face. Art is not Art when it is not consistent.

When you said "a book about the operas" did you mean a book you wrote? Of course I would like to read it. First time the wagon goes to town let the book come along, will you? Down in Texas at one time I belonged to a first rate musical association (Amateur). We toured the State with Pinafore & the Bohemian Girl & the Black Mantles & the Mikado & the "Chimes" &c. Me? Oh, in the chorus, of course. Except once. Sang the part of Don Hypolito Lopez Pomposo Antonio Riccardo Doloroso in the Black Mantles. I put in the next 2 years living it down, & finally succeeded.

Wait a minute 'till I look at that little 2 x 4 letter of yours. O!

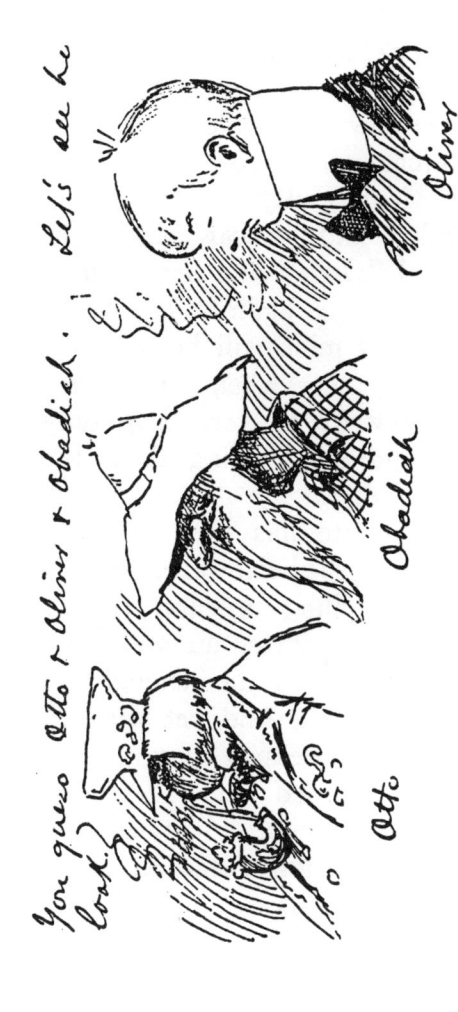

A facsimile reproduction of the sketches of "Otto," "Obadiah," and "Oliver"

LETTERS TO

That's not an exclamation. You guess Otto & Oliver & Obadiah. Let's see how they look [see page 27 for sketches that accompanied this letter]. Not guilty. Why there's "Orlando" and "Oscar" and "Orville" and "Osric" and heaps more.

Now, let's see again. The book! that book of mine will be out—it's hard to say just when. I haven't begun to write it yet. I've only gotten as far as deciding about the cover and edges.

I think Fate has been unjustly kind to you in the bestowal of favours. You are revelling in rural felicity and eggs and country air and scenery. That should be enough to satisfy any one. And yet with all those blessings heaped at your feet you are accorded the additional privilege of having witnessed the thrilling destruction of Bart Kramer's

LITHOPOLIS

barn by the fire demon. It is not fair. Isn't a holiday enough for you without your demanding holocausts too? Though denied the spectacle myself, I can imagine the exciting scene—the lurid flames lighting up the lurid heavens with their lurid glare, and Bart rarin' and chargin' around trying to rescue the buggy harness and the settin' hen. In such supreme moments do you never give a thought to the unfortunates cooped up in the city with nothing to entertain them except roof gardens & murders and the new guimpe styles in piqué & Russian blouses?

I'm awfully obliged for the nice things you said about my little old stories. I don't think very much of 'em myself, but it sounds kind of friendly, anyway. The only line in which I am convinced that I am truly great is in Art. This you can see

LETTERS

for yourself. I once illustrated a book for a Texas writer. When he saw the pictures he tore up his MS and threw it into the Colorado river. That's a fact.

I suppose this nonsense of mine is getting to be a nuisance by this time. But I really am not able to take things solemnly. The whole business —life, literature, operas, philosophy & shirt waists—is a kind of a joke, isn't it? I reckon that riding around on a pony on the Texas prairies thinking about the beans and barbecued beef we're going to have for supper is about as good as anything. When the illusions go the best thing to do is to take it good-humouredly. So, there's some philosophy for you. It isn't solid enough to keep you awake after the frogs begin to croak in Lithopolis.

I'm thinking of running down to

Sketch of Lithopolis, from the letter of July 23, 1903

LETTERS TO

Tennessee for a little vacation next month. The mountains for me! Don't you think mountains are real cute? Won't you write me again before then & say au revoir? And tell me—is the tombstone lady doing nicely? And did Bart have any insurance? And are there any katydids? And crickets? But don't telegraph. Letter by first mail will relieve anxiety.

Yours very sincerely
O. Henry.

IV

INTRODUCTORY NOTE

O. Henry was continually sending me magazine stories—either recently, formerly, or about to be, published. They all attested to his rapid advance on the road to fame, and, being only human, I could not resist the impulse to send something myself to show

LITHOPOLIS

that I, in my own poor way, was snailing along that same deep-rutted, long long road. I mailed him a copy of my book "Miserere," and deftly, sort of careless-like, slipped in among the pages a circular of press notices about my concert work. All of which accounts for the slam-bang jollying I get in the following letter.

The Storekeeper incident is a more intricate matter to explain. It involves, I am sorry to say, a little side-stepping on my part from the rigid line of veracity which the four churches of Lithopolis were aiming to inculcate. It happened in this way: One day at the drug store, where the books on one side balanced the bottles on the other, I was looking over the magazines and found one of them featuring on the cover a story by O. Henry. So conspicuous was the

LETTERS TO

name that Mr. Bennett, the compounder of drugs and dispenser of books, had noticed and read the story. He was one who, in spite of his pill-boxes, thought more of mind than of matter. In reply to a pride-prompted statement from me that I knew O. Henry—had had several letters from him—he regarded me with sudden interest and exclaimed:

"You don't say! How did you come to know him?"

This was a question I was unprepared for: in fact, I never have found myself fully accoutred—armed *cap-à-pie*—to parry this shaft when flung at me suddenly. When divorced from its adjacent incidents, the simple statement of fact, "I wrote a letter and asked who he was," is a statement that might go unchallenged in Greenwich Village, but would hardly pass in Lithopolis.

LITHOPOLIS

When flustered one clutches at half truths.

"He is a distant cousin of my great grandmother," I announced with an air of finality that quieted the storekeeper's curiosity and also my own conscience, for I still did not know that the Henry name was fictitious, and as I had not specified the distance of the cousinship my statement could stand firm under considerable bombardment. My great grandmother's name was Hannah Henry—upon this foundation rock of fact I stood unbudging as one of Alta Jungkurth's stones.

So much for the "hazardous" incident with the Storekeeper.

M. W.

LETTERS TO

O. HENRY
TO MISS WAGNALLS

New York, Sept. 7th, 1903.

MY DEAR MISS WAGNALLS:

I RETURNED to N. Y. this week from a visit to —— Tennessee? No, Pittsburg!!!! (Thank you for the sympathy expressed upon your countenance.) Smoke, soot, gloom, rain, hordes of Philistines and money-changers in all the temples—well, you know what it was like. There is a new, popular version of the poem commemorative of the diminutive incipient sheep whose outer covering was as devoid of colour as congealed atmospheric vapour of whom Mary was the proprietress that seems not to do the subject injustice. Have you heard it? It runs this way:

"Mary had a little lamb;
    Its fleece was white as snow;
    She took it to Pittsburg one day—

LITHOPOLIS

And you just ought to see the gol
darned thing now!"

I read with much interest the little collection of press notices that you enclosed. Besides a lot of other things it tells me the old story of woman's duplicity. I thought of you as a simple Manhattan maiden in Lithopolis killing caterpillars in a white Leghorn hat (not killing 'em in the hat) while you plucked daffodils and related to an admiring peasantry the glories of the Eden Musée & Macy's Store. And then, without a moment's warning, you hurl at me the information that fame is yours—the real stuff with laurel trimmings and bay insertion—that your grosses entwicklungsfähiges talent made 'em sit up & take notice in Berlin, and the Schulerleistung knocked 'em cold in Plattsburg, N.Y.

LETTERS TO

But, really, I do realize what a success you have made, and I congratulates you most heartily, although you've made me feel quite small and unimportant. Oh, what an exquisite, rippling allegro, staccato little "jolly" you have been giving me! Telling me nice things about my poor little stories, when all the time you were getting bouquets in Berlin and "bravas" in Binghampton and curtain calls in Conewago and—well, I'm real mad—so, there!

I will try to forgive you for trapping me so neatly by asking me so demurely and offhandishly if I was interested in music. I was sure that you were going to say next time that you and your school chum had arranged "Hiawatha" for a duet, and that you could play the "Battle of Prague" with your wrists crossed—and then comes this D minor con-

LITHOPOLIS

certo opus 47 news and strikes me right between the eyes. I have taken the full count. I do not know a concerto or a legato from a perfecto or a tomato, but I can recognize success, and if you will please listen carefully you will hear some hand-clapping 'way up in the peanut gallery—and that'll be *me*.

I read "Miserere," which you so kindly sent, with no small interest. I fancy that it is intended to appeal rather to those who possess the musical temperament and enthusiasm. I am barred out from the peculiar region in which the soul of the musician is supposed to dwell, but I found the tale ingenious and pleasing, and admired the contained and simple style in which it is told. It seemed to me to be a natural and unstudied expression. If it was art it is good art; but you will please keep on your

LETTERS TO

own ground and don't come interfering with my line of business. I don't try to compete with you in your opuses and things, and I think you ought to play fair. I did take a course of Sep Winner's System of Self-Instruction for the Violin in the woodshed at home, but I am not continuing it at present, so I do not feel that you could consider your laurels in any danger from me. Lawsy! ain't it funny how much jealousy there is between us artists?

Now, Miss Wagnalls, will you allow me to use a poetic phrase and ask you to quit your kiddin'? Unless you are really doing so (and I grieve, yea, I drop a tear to think so) you must know that I haven't nearly "arrived" yet. I'm only on the road, and the "meteor" and "comet" & "fixed star" that you make believe you see is only the milky way,

LITHOPOLIS

and very skim-milky at that, and you have very kindly put on a pair of your grandma's magnifying glasses to view it with.

Now, if you don't quit it, when I write again I'll fill every page with extremely laudatory praise of the way you sledgehammered that nocturne solfeggio of Chopin's in G flat in the opera house at Rahway, N. J.

What a very hazardous situation you were in when you had the conversation with the storekeeper! How fortunate that you were not called upon to give him a description of your grandmother's vague & mysterious, not to say suspicious relative. Out of concern for your feelings, in a future predicament, I feel that I ought to furnish you with means of extrication from it. Should you happen to go "up to the store" again and meet an inquiry of a similar nature, just

LETTERS TO

lay the enclosed counterfeit presentment (clipped from a catalogue) on the counter, and say: "that's him." Be sure to say "him." You might lay the picture close against the gumdrop jar as you do so, thus giving the storekeeper a chance to remark: "Well, by gum!"

If the storekeeper here should ask me about the distinguished pianist whom I am so proud to know so slightly, of course I would be utterly silenced and confounded. I could only bow my head with regret and humiliation, and walk out of the store. I could lay nothing next to the gumdrop jar in silent but happy confirmation of my claims.

Ah, well, of course I could not expect—but—well,—would there—I mean—I know there couldn't—but—well, if—(I guess I'll have to correct this sentence in the proofs). But

LITHOPOLIS

a bright idea strikes me! Aha! Genius can scarcely escape belonging, to a certain extent, to the public. Maybe there is one in a book. Aha! away to the Astor library to search the musical publications! Even yet I may hurl against the gumdrop jar a heavy volume containing it! A good title for a story—"The Possessed Picture, or the Penalty of Playing the Piano in Public."

Very glad you wrote again. I enjoy your letters very much, only they are too brief.

Sincerely yours
O. HENRY.

V

INTRODUCTORY NOTE

THE substance of the next letter was called forth by one from me announcing our intended return to New York.

LETTERS TO

The clipping from the "Reader" magazine was a brief biography about "the new luminary in fiction's firmament." It was the first article, I believe, revealing that O. Henry was the *nom de plume* of Sydney Porter.

                                M. W.

O. HENRY
TO MISS WAGNALLS

44 West 26th St.
New York, Oct. 13 [1903].

MY DEAR MISS WAGNALLS:

"'THE time has come,' the walrus said, 'to talk of many things.'" I have a deep, dark confession to make to you. Please consider me kneeling before you with one knee on a handkerchief, and the orchestra playing: "Since first I met you."

If you remember, once you wrote that you did not know whether I were "man, woman or wraith."

LITHOPOLIS

Well, I am a wraith. There never was an "O. Henry." The name is a *nom de guerre;* but still it is mine, for I made it.

While I do not claim to be specially modest or violet-like, I have always disliked publicity, and therefore I have written and often corresponded with publishers and others above that pseudonym.

The clipping from the "Reader" which I enclose will serve to further illuminate the matter.

Of course, to the editors of "McClure's" and "Ainslee's" and "Everybody's," "Harper's," &c., I am known personally, and they assist me in preserving the pen name.

Yes, indeed, Miss; and if ye wants any riferences, ye can ask them same gintlemen, sure, what they knows about "O. Hinry."

LETTERS TO

I hope you won't consider my "Henry" rôle as anything like a deception, for I began writing to you that way and—well I AM "O. HENRY," so maybe you'll let me stay so. I'm sure I'd rather be your cousin than anybody else's I know.

Indeed I would be very glad and pleased to call at your home as you have so graciously extended permission, and if you decide, after reading my confession of guilt, to allow me to do so, I will look forward to the time with much pleasure.

I read with some alarm your threats with regard to the "new frock." Please don't do it. I'm only a lone cowpuncher—a long ways from camp, and I shy like a bronco at anything with passementerie or ruching on the flounces. Please make it a quiet, soothing function—

LITHOPOLIS

just as the boys and girls meet in the graveyard in Lithopolis—won't you?

I'd like very much to come down and tell you all about tarantulas and cyclones and train robbers &c.

If you decide to forgive me for my (innocent) deception, please notify me, and I will feel happier.

No, I am not as busy as you think. I should be, but as I have no one to boss me and make me keep at work I am generally what you would call pretty lazy. Therefore, my evenings are mostly open, as most of my movements are decidedly impromptu.

So, if I am so lucky as to escape your censure, I would esteem it a great favour to be allowed to call any evening—say Thursday or Friday this week or any evening next week, whichever may suit you best.

If you decide to "turn down" the

LETTERS TO

"wraith" there will be no more calendar—neither days, weeks, or months.

    Sincerely yours
& hoping to be still your cousin
    SYDNEY PORTER
      "O. HENRY."

—

VI

INTRODUCTORY NOTE

THIS "Majesty" letter has back of it considerable language in the way of conversation—as the Gentle Grafter would say.

We had talked once of the impossible manuscripts that are sent to and passed through every editorial sanctum. He told of spending an hour with an editor who was glancing over the day's accumulation of stories, one of which, in describing a social function, said:

LITHOPOLIS

"The rooms were filled by——"

O. Henry paused at this point and asked me to guess what they were filled by. I gave it up: "by half-past nine" was the conclusion of the quotation.

I contributed a phrase gleaned from a Funk & Wagnalls MS. that had come our way: it was a novel dealing with Anne of Austria. The Duke of Buckingham had addressed Her Majesty with some query—I forget what—but the next line read:

"'Sure,' said the Queen."

Some time later I read a story by Rex Beach—a new name in those days—and finding a touch of the Henryesque in the style, and recalling that O. Henry had told me he sometimes wrote stories under other names, I jumped to the conclusion that this was one of them. Crossing out the Rex Beach name and writing O.

LETTERS TO

Henry above it, I added as sole explanation, the words "'Sure,' said the Queen." The day after mailing him the story I received this royal reply. M. W.

O. HENRY
TO MISS WAGNALLS

25 East 24th St.,
N. Y. Nov. 11 [1903].

TO HER MAJESTY
THE
QUEEN OF BAD GUESSERS

"WRONG, your Majesty," replied the thingumbob.

Rather funny, but Rex E. Beach called in to see me just after I had your royal communication. He is a big, broad, breezy fellow from Alaska, and he travels for a fire brick manufactory, and writes his stories on trains or pieces of paper or whatever comes handy.

LITHOPOLIS

Here I am at 25 E 24th, and 3 editors are guarding the door & keeping me in at work.

Won't your Majesty send a troop of Mousquetaires to rescue me?

I'm as ragged and disreputable looking as Russell Sage. When I sell a story & buy some new clothes may I then ask you to give me some more tea?

P. S. And little cakes. Yours very truly and hard at work

O. H.

VII

INTRODUCTORY NOTE

ANOTHER painful incident, similar to the one that occurred in Mr. Bennett's drug store, was the occasion for this diatribe upon the crime of prevarication. A stranger whom I met at a reception was the villain in this instance who cast me into confusion and blighted my expanding pride in O. Henry's acquaintance.

"How did you happen to meet him?" I suddenly heard thundered at me. The man may have spoken mildly, but those words were to me like a bomb from the blue. I was not wholly paralyzed, however, and therefore succeeded in answering vaguely but rather ingenuously, I think, and with a commendable regard for the half-truth:

"Oh, through an editor friend."

The villain's next sentence explained the why of his interest in my meeting with the Lone Star of Texas. He (the villain) also hailed from that state, and having cowboy memories akin to O. Henry's had frequently thought of trying to lasso an acquaintanceship with him. In fact, he stated his intention of proceeding

LITHOPOLIS

at once to look him up. I instantly had visions of a chummy intimacy ensuing between O. Henry and the villain, and the possibility that he might learn that not an editor friend but a letter of curiosity from me had started up our acquaintance. One does hate to be caught in a—mistruth. Rather than be caught in it, one prefers owning up in advance. So this is what I did—wrote out a full confession, which I signed and sealed and sent to O. Henry—with fine results, as every reader of the following letter will admit.

O. HENRY
TO MISS WAGNALLS

[Date on Envelope Dec. 8, 1903.]
    25 E 24th St.,
       New York.

MY DEAR MISS WAGNALLS:

You can't imagine how delighted I am to welcome you, as an honorary

LETTERS TO

Member, into the noble army of Prevaricators. I am one by preference, habit, and practice, and I have an unholy glee whenever we get in a recruit from the rapidly thinning ranks of the Truth Tellers.

Of course I will protect your retreat from that very dull company; and if the "terrible person from Texas" dares to propound any of his impertinent interrogations, I shall swear to him by the eye-tooth of Ananias in the sacred Lodge Room of the Prevaricators that Mr. Wheeler was so kind as to introduce me to you at a tea party at half past five under an oleander tree in the prairie during a snowstorm in July while you wore a pink chiffon overcoat and an organdie muff just after a cattle round-up in Madison Avenue. These little details will give the story—watch out for this word—verisimilitude, won't they?

LITHOPOLIS

But don't let your conscience bother you, you did exactly right. Next time it will be much easier, and by and by you will become a full-fledged member of the P's, and can tell 'em just as easy!

I suppose, with your unfortunate love for music, that you are enjoying the extremely disagreeable noises with which the alleged operas are delighting the misguided admirers of such sounds this season. I, myself, have never heard "Tannhäuser" or "Aïda," but I do not wish to seem as boasting of my luck. Of course I'm not saying anything against the piano. Before the pianola was invented the piano was a real joy and convenience in homes where nobody could play it—they're so handy to pile old magazines on.

Do you ever hear from Lithopolis? Sitting here in my lonely apartments

LETTERS TO

(1) I often wonder if Bart Kramer has rebuilt his barn yet—the one devastated by the fearful holocaust that struck its ice-cold fangs into the doomed city while you were there. And again I sit in the gloaming and seem to see the patient figure of Jane Harkishamer as she fetches up the hoss and buggy to the gate. And the tombstone lady!—is she still settin' 'em up to her friends yet?

I'm afraid you're fickle, and you now prefer Rex E. Beach and Marietta Holly, or you would keep me posted about these matters in which we were once mutually interested. Aha! Do I see you turn pale? You are discovered! Once your Cousin but now forgotten!!

"O Henry."

LITHOPOLIS

VIII

THIS letter is almost self-explanatory. The book, sent through my publishers, is dedicated:

"To those who love music but have no
opportunity of familiarizing themselves
with Grand Opera."

O. Henry, with his characteristic cleverness in juggling phrases, wittily inverts my dedication.

M. W.

O. HENRY
TO MISS WAGNALLS

28 West 26th Street,
New York, Oct. 28, 1907.

MY DEAR MISS WAGNALLS:

YOUR publishers sent me your latest book some days ago, and your card accompanying it leads me to suspect that you instigated the deed.

I am sure proud to get it; and have

LETTERS

waited a few days before writing in order to send with my acknowledgment my latest volume of poor, insignificant, tiresome, unworthy, dull, pusillanimous, insufferable stories.

(Of course you understand that the adjectives are hypocritical.)

I am going to read "Stars of the Opera" carefully, and use the information in my conversation to gain a "rep" as a musical critic without having to go through the work of listening to the music.

I feel that I am one of the dedicatees of your book, and that the printer has been in error, and that it should read "To those who love musicians but have no opportunity to familiarize themselves with writers on grand opera."

Oh, those proof-readers!

Sincerely yours
SYDNEY PORTER.

THIS VOLUME WAS PRINTED BY
DOUBLEDAY, PAGE & COMPANY
AT THE COUNTRY LIFE PRESS
GARDEN CITY, LONG ISLAND, N. Y.
THE PRINTING WAS COMPLETED IN
THE MONTH OF FEBRUARY
MCMXXII

ABOUT MABEL WAGNALLS

The letters contained in this volume had two authors—O. Henry and Mabel Wagnalls. Miss Wagnalls not only initiated the correspondence, but recognizing the talent he was displaying in the many stories he was publishing, she preserved and eventually published the letters she received.

The reader familiar with O. Henry's style may note stylistic devices in her writing which reflect her mentor's touch. Whether these traces of style were reflected in her original letters, or whether they came into her writing as she retold the story, cannot be discerned. If they were her own, such delightful originality may have been one of the reasons O. Henry replied to her first letter and continued the exchange through the summer of 1903 and beyond.

In her early letters, modestly presenting herself merely as the daughter of the Wagnalls of the publishing firm of Funk and Wagnalls, she apparently compared him to a meteor or fixed star, while she considered herself a long way from having "arrived." She did not for some time mention that she was also a published writer. Eventually, as she admits in an introduction to one of the letters, she did confess to her literary ambitions and even sent a copy of her novel, *Miserere*. In commenting on the

About Mabel Wagnalls

novel, O. Henry offered neither praise nor suggestions, saying merely that he "found the tale ingenious and pleasing and admired the contained and simple style in which it is told.... If it was art it is good art." In response to some press notices she had slipped in about her keyboard performances, he disclaimed having enough knowledge of music to comment.*

As a matter of record, Mabel Wagnall's *Miserere*, published when she was in her early twenties, reflects the late Victorian society of which she was so much a part: the stylized manners, the fears, the love of beauty, the formulaic sudden and tragic death. The same Victorian values are revealed in her great fear that someone might discover that she had not been properly introduced to O. Henry, although she had occasionally and deliberately let the information drop that she had been corresponding with him.

It will also be noted that she displayed a deep appreciation and knowledge of classical music, a love evident throughout the book from its opera-

---

*As a youth in North Carolina and later in his Austin years, William Sydney Porter had displayed a natural musical talent. He possessed a deep baritone voice, sang in amateur light opera, church choirs, and a well-known Austin quartet. His daughter Margaret found his piano playing, done only for her and no other audience that she ever knew of, quite lovely. During his New York years, especially after his editors were always breathing down his neck, he had no time for music, or even, as some of his friends noted, for much reading.

About Mabel Wagnalls

based title to the theme of the individuality of one beautiful voice.

By contrast, *Stars of the Opera*, which has a copyright date of 1899 and publication date of 1907, features interviews which Miss Wagnalls held with women of the European, English, and American opera. The stars interviewed are hardly remembered today, but they created roles in new operas that were being written in the late nineteenth century, beginning with *La Traviata* as it was performed in the new Metropolitan Opera House. Marcella Sembrich, who played in thirty-seven operas and was fluent in "all the continental languages," heads the parade, which includes Emma Earnes, Ema Calve, Lillian Nordica, Lilli Lehmann, Geraline Farrar, and Nellie Melba. Introducing the stars' roles in operas still played lends a familiarity to persons whose names are now all but unknown, and Wagnalls' criticism brings new life to the operas at the end of another century.

But even more interesting is the fact that one hundred years ago a woman writer put in perspective the careers of seven women, born at widely differing spots in the world, who carved places for women in what she considered "the finest of the classical arts." Along the way, she explains the plots and music of operas popular one hundred years ago which make up much of today's repertoire. And she puts it all in language that is as current today as the music itself—a special talent for one who would dedicate a book of serious criticism

About Mabel Wagnalls

To those who love music but have
No opportunity to familiarize
themselves with grand opera . . .

Like the letters to Lithopolis, Mabel Wagnalls
deserves a place in musical and literary history.

> Vi Marie Taylor
> Austin, Texas
> November 5, 1999